# BOORAN

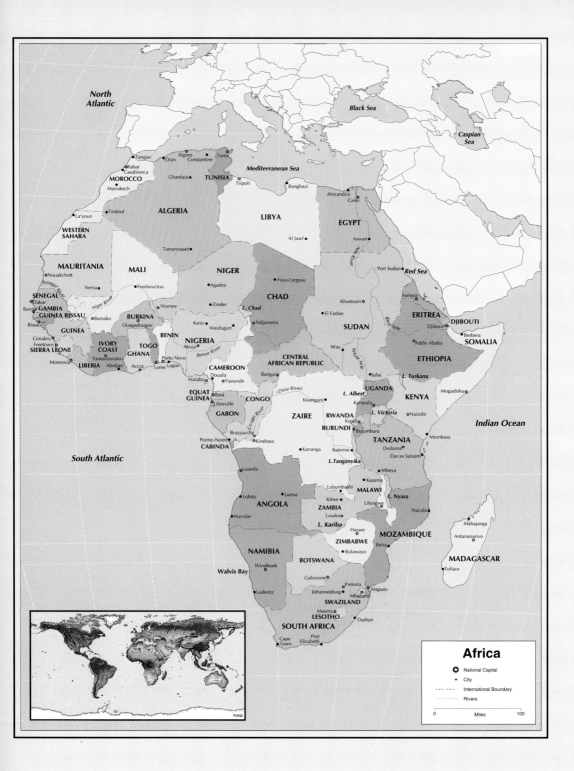

**North Atlantic**

**Black Sea**

**Caspian Sea**

Tangier • ● Algiers Tunis
Rabat ● Oran ● Constantine ● **Mediterranean Sea**
Casablanca
**MOROCCO** Ghardaia ● **TUNISIA** Tripoli ●
Marrakech ● Banghazi ●
Alexandria ●
La'youn ● Tindouf ● Cairo ●
**ALGERIA** **LIBYA** **EGYPT**
**WESTERN SAHARA**
Al Jawf ● Aswan ●
Tamanrasset ●
Port Sudan ● **Red Sea**
**MAURITANIA** **MALI** **NIGER**
Nouakchott ● Asmera ●
Nema ● Tombouctou ● Agadez ● Faya-Largeau ● Khartoum ● **ERITREA**
**SENEGAL** Zinder ● **CHAD** Djibouti ● **DJIBOUTI**
Dakar ● Niamey ● L. Chad El Fasher ●
Banjul ● **GAMBIA** Bamako ● Kano ● **SUDAN** Berbera ●
**GUINEA BISSAU** Ouagadougou ● Maiduguri ● Ndjamena ● Addis Ababa ● **SOMALIA**
Bissau ● **BURKINA** Wau ● **ETHIOPIA**
Conakry ● **GUINEA** **BENIN** **NIGERIA** Benue River Mogadishu ●
Freetown ● **IVORY** **TOGO** Abuja ● **CENTRAL** **L. Turkana**
**SIERRA LEONE** **COAST** **GHANA** **AFRICAN REPUBLIC**
Monrovia ● Yamoussoukro Porto Novo Bangui ● Juba ● **KENYA**
**LIBERIA** Abidjan ● Accra ● Lagos **CAMEROON** **UGANDA**
Lome Douala ● L. Albert Nairobi ●
Malabo ● Yaounde ● Kisangani ● Kampala ●
**EQUAT.** Bata ● (Zaire River) L. Victoria **KENYA**
**GUINEA** Libreville ● **CONGO** **RWANDA** Kigali ●
**South Atlantic** **GABON** **ZAIRE** **BURUNDI** Bujumbura ● Mombasa ●
Pointe-Noire ● Brazzaville ● **TANZANIA** **Indian Ocean**
**CABINDA** Kinshasa ● Kananga ● Dodoma ●
Kalemie ● Dar es Salaam ●
Luanda ● L.Tanganyika
Mbeya ●
Kasama ●
Lobito ● Luena ● Lubumbashi ● **MALAWI**
**ANGOLA** Kitwe ● Lilongwe ● **L. Nyasa**
Namibe ● **ZAMBIA** Lusaka ● Nacala ●
L. Kariba
Harare ● **MOZAMBIQUE**
**NAMIBIA** **ZIMBABWE** Beira ●
**Walvis Bay** **BOTSWANA** Bulawayo ● **MADAGASCAR**
Mahajanga ●
Windhoek ● Antananarivo ●
Gaborone ●
Luderitz ● Pretoria ● Maputo ●
Johannesburg ● Mbabane ● Toliara ●
**SWAZILAND**
Maseru ● **LESOTHO**
**SOUTH AFRICA** Durban ●
Cape Town ● Port Elizabeth ●

## Africa

✪ National Capital
● City
– – – International Boundary
— Rivers

0     Miles     100

The Heritage Library of African Peoples

# BOORAN

Gemetchu Megerssa, Ph.D.

THE ROSEN PUBLISHING GROUP, INC.
NEW YORK

Published in 1995 by The Rosen Publishing Group, Inc.
29 East 21st Street, New York, NY 10010

First Edition

Manufactured in the United States of America

**Library of Congress Cataloging-in-Publication Data**

Megerssa, Gemetchu.
    Booran / Gemetchu Megerssa.
      p.  cm. — (Heritage library of African peoples)
    Includes bibliographical references and index.
    ISBN 0-8239-1769-X
    1. Boran (African people)—Juvenile literature.  [1. Boran
(African people)]  I. Title.  II. Series.
DT433.545.B67M44  1995
967.62′004935—dc20                95-8473
                                     CIP
                                     AC

# Contents

# INTRODUCTION

**THERE IS EVERY REASON FOR US TO KNOW** something about Africa and to understand its past and the way of life of its peoples. Africa is a rich continent that has for centuries provided the world with art, culture, labor, wealth, and natural resources. It has vast mineral deposits, fossil fuels, and commercial crops.

But perhaps most important is the fact that fossil evidence indicates that human beings originated in Africa. The earliest traces of human beings and their tools are almost two million years old. Their descendants have migrated throughout the world. To be human is to be of African descent.

The experiences of the peoples who stayed in Africa are as rich and as diverse as of those who established themselves elsewhere. This series of books describes their environment, their modes of subsistence, their relationships, and their customs and beliefs. The books present the variety of languages, histories, cultures, and religions that are to be found on the African continent. They demonstrate the historical linkages between African peoples and the way contemporary Africa has been affected by European colonial rule.

Africa is large, complex, and diverse. It encompasses an area of more than 11,700,000

square miles. The United States, Europe, and India could fit easily into it. The sheer size is an indication of the continent's great variety in geography, terrain, climate, flora, fauna, peoples, languages, and cultures.

Much of contemporary Africa has been shaped by European colonial rule, industrialization, urbanization, and the demands of a world economic system. For more than seventy years, large regions of Africa were ruled by Great Britain, France, Belgium, Portugal, and Spain. African peoples from various ethnic, linguistic, and cultural backgrounds were brought together to form colonial states.

For decades Africans struggled to gain their independence. It was not until after World War II that the colonial territories become independent African states. Today, almost all of Africa is ruled by Africans. Large numbers of Africans live in modern cities. Rural Africa is also being transformed, and yet its people still engage in many of their age-old customs and beliefs.

Contemporary circumstances and natural events have not always been kind to ordinary Africans. Today, however, new popular social movements and technological innovations pose great promise for future development.

George C. Bond, Ph.D., Director
Institute of African Studies
Columbia University, New York

The Booran belong to the larger group called Oromo.

chapter

# 1

# THE BOORAN PEOPLE

*LONG AGO THERE WAS NO TIME, THERE WAS NO day, there was no night. Only the creator Waaqa existed. Waaqa wanted all that was contained in himself to come into being. But he knew that he first had to give life to all things. Waaqa also knew that water was the source of all life. And so he created a body of water. He called this water Horra Wallaabu, that which is impregnated with life. In this body of water Waaqa placed the seed of all things. Waaqa then began the work of creation. He began to bring forth the world. He divided the impregnated body of water into two parts: the waters of the Above (Biaan Gubbaa) and the Waters of the Below (Bisaan Goddaa). He divided the Waters of the Above into three parts: water, sky, and heavenly bodies. The Waters of the Below he divided into two parts: water and earth. Waaqa named these five acts of creation the Yaayaa Shanaan, or the five*

*fundaments. With these, Waaqa drew the ground
plan upon which the rest of the world would be built.*

*Time began with the birth of the sun and the
moon. The first day began when the sun rose at
dawn and ended when the sun set on the first night.
This first day Waaqa called* addula, *meaning "first
sun."*

*It took Waaqa 27 days to complete his creation.
In this time, he created all the things that are to be
found in the heavens, in the earth, and all those
things that float in the air and swim in the water.
The things that Waaqa created in heaven were made
in one dawn. The things on earth took two dawns to
be completed, and those in the air and in the water
took three dawns. These 27 days occurred between
the rising and setting of two new moons. Every tenth
day, the creator rested, and so he took three days off.*

*Then Waaqa made humans. Waaqa named the
first man Horo. On Horo's body Waaqa placed five
limbs, a head, two arms, and two legs. Each hand
divided into five fingers and each foot divided into
five toes. On his face Waaqa placed seven features.
Horo thus reflected Waaqa's period of creation, because he was made up of 27 different parts. On the
body of the human being, three parts remain
unaccounted, corresponding to the three days in
which the creation of the world remained suspended.*

The people known today as the Booran did
not exist as a separate people until the beginning

A Booran warrior wearing traditional clothing and weapons.

of the twentieth century. Before this time, they formed part of a larger nation known as the Oromo. The above tale is a myth, passed down from generation to generation, explaining how the Oromo people came into being. The Oromo belong to an ancient people known as the

Booran women with their children relaxing in the early afternoon.

Cushites. Although the exact origins of the Cushites are unknown, through their language and culture they are thought to be related to the ancient Egyptians.

The Oromo language belongs to the Afro-Asiatic family of languages and more specifically to the Eastern Cushitic group. Oromo is said to be the second-largest indigenous language in Africa and is spoken in a vast area in East Africa. It is estimated that between 25 and 30 million Oromo people speak this language. Now split by international boundaries, Oromoland

stretches from the Red Sea in Ethiopia in the north, to Mombasa, Kenya, on the Indian Ocean to the south, encompassing parts of Somalia to the east and bordering the Sudan to the west.

### ▼ THE ORIGINS OF THE OROMO ▼

The Oromo trace their descent from Horo, the founding father. In the Oromo language, the name Horo comes from the verb *horu*, meaning to multiply and be fertile. The first letter "h" is not always pronounced, and so the name (H)Oromo means the people who were descended from Horo.

According to the Oromo myth of descent, Horo, the founding father, had two sons. His firstborn son was named Booran; his younger son was named Barrentu. In Oromo language, the word *booro* designates the wall of the back or bedroom of the traditional Oromo house. The entrance of the house, from the inside looking out, traditionally faces the east. The rays of the rising sun pass through the eastern opening of the house to the room where the head of the household sleeps. The word *anna* means "toward" or "next to." In the Oromo language, the last vowel is not always pronounced. The two parts of the name "Booran(a)" together mean "those who face the east," the source of light and the origin of all life. Similarly, the name Barrentu is made up of two terms: *barrii*, meaning sunrise, and -*aantu*, the feminine form of -*anna*. Together the words signify "those facing the west."

According to the oral traditions of the origins of the Oromo nation, Booran married three wives, each of whom bore him a son. Barrentu married two wives, who also each bore him a male child. The five sons of Booran and Barrentu spread in five directions and founded the five territories of traditional Oromoland. The descendants of Booran's sons each divided into two groups: the Raaya and Assebu, the Macha and Tullama, and the Sabbo and Goona. These are the Oromo groups who are today in the western part of Oromoland. The descendants of Barrentu's sons also each divided into two groups: the Ittu and Humbana and the Sikko and Mando. These divisions of the Oromo are in the eastern part of Oromoland.

All the groups descended from Booran were collectively known as Booran. All those groups descended from Barrentu were collectively known as Barrentu. The Booran and Barrentu formed the two halves of the Oromo nation, divided into its western and eastern branches. This division is marked by the Great Rift Valley, which crosses Oromoland and forms a natural barrier between the eastern and western parts of its territory.

The name Booran is used as a generic term

for all the western Oromo groups, while Barrentu designates the eastern groups.

### ▼ THE MEANING OF BOORAN ▼

The name Booran has more than one meaning. It refers to the people descended from the eldest son of Horo. It also stands for the ideal of elderhood as represented by the firstborn son. The overall Oromo society is categorized in two basic ways. It is first divided into two groups, the Booran (those living in the east) and the Barrentu (those living in the west). Then it is further divided into the Booran (the elders of society) and the Gabaro (the juniors of society).

### ▼ OROMO SOCIETY ▼

The traditional Oromo society used a complex system to classify all the living and nonliving things in its cultural universe. One basic concept in this system was that the firstborn son is by nature superior to all those sons born after him. The Oromo extended this privilege not only to actual firstborn sons, but also to all their descendants. The notion of elderhood served as a method for classifying the different groups that made up the Oromo nation. Positive value was attached to the eldest son because his position was unique. This distinction between elder and junior thus served as a means of dividing the society into several levels

One basic concept in Oromo society is that the firstborn son is by nature superior to all the sons born after him.

and of marking social, economic, political, and religious differences.

Traditional Oromo society was seen as a larger version of a family. All firstborn sons in the family were known as Booran; all other sons were known as Gabaro (the names Garba or Gabra are also used, depending on the region). So, in addition to the other meanings of the term Booran, it also describes the relationship between the elder and younger brothers in the Oromo family structure. Booranhood was the birthright that could be claimed by the eldest son, regardless of whether he was Booran or Barrentu. Superior status and prestige were attributed to the eldest son. It was also the means through which wealth and power were regulated.

The eldest son inherited the family property at the death of his father and succeeded him as the head of the household. He was also expected to replace his father as the ritual head of the family and to perform the necessary ceremonies and sacrifices. The eldest son was therefore taught from early childhood to assume this position of responsibility. He and other elder sons received a specialized education. Power was concentrated in a small elite of elder sons. The Booran became the dominant group in the society.

This position of power was idealized. The Oromo believed that the firstborn son opened

the passage through his mother's womb, ena-
bling his younger brothers to come into the
world. The firstborn son was therefore the chan-
nel through whom all life flowed. He was the
most blessed child, the child sacred to Waaqa,
the creator. The Booran were said to have a
black tongue, the color of Waaqa. They had the
absolute power to bless or curse.

The Booran elder sons were physically distin-
guished from other members of the society by
wearing a unique hairstyle and special ornaments. The "true" or "pure" Booran were
known as the *Booran guutuu*, or those who wore
a tuft of hair on the crown of their heads.
Booran leaders carried and wore certain sacred
objects that gave them mystical force. Their high
social rank also obliged them to follow a code of
moral conduct on behalf of the entire society.
This included following food taboos and maintaining the right posture and demeanor, as well
as displaying moderation in speech.

These beliefs and responsibilities legitimized
the economic dominance of the eldest sons. All
land was said to be owned by the Booran, who
took possession of it on behalf of all the people.
Land could be given to the Gabaro only by the
Booran, who were responsible for blessing it. In
order to be closest to Waaqa and to offer sacri-
ficial gifts to the creator on high places, Booran
lived on the most elevated ground. This gener-

Booran elders dressed in traditional clothing.

ally corresponded to the most fertile country in the cool highlands of Oromoland, where agriculture could be practiced and where the most prestigious livestock, cattle, could be raised. The younger Gabaro brothers were therefore forced to live in the lowlands of Oromo country and to lead a less privileged life.

In these low-lying lands, the Gabaro served as the rear guard in the military defense of the Oromo territory. In their position as frontiersmen, the Gabaro were more exposed to influences from people living on the lands bordering Oromo territory. As a result of contact with other cultures, the Gabaro groups acquired dif-

19

The Gabaro or Gabra brothers led less privileged lives in the lowlands.

ferences in speech, dress, and other cultural features, while at the same time retaining the essence of their Oromoness. These differences and the conceptual distinction between the Booran and Gabaro were misunderstood by British colonists in the early 20th century, who mistook the Gabaro for a completely separate group from the Booran.

### ▼ THE SABBO AND GOONA BOORAN OROMO ▼

The people known to the world today as the "Booran" belong more precisely to the Sabbo and Goona groups that made up one of the five territorial divisions of the Oromo nation. Today,

the two groups are known simply as the Booran. That name was applied to them by British and Abyssinian colonial administrators at the beginning of the 20th century. The British designated "tribal grazing areas" in Kenya in 1909. By doing this they intentionally separated the highland cattle-keeping Booran from the lowland camel-keeping Gabra within the Sabbo and Goona groups. From this time onward, following the colonial policy of divide and rule, they became known as distinct "tribes." The main Booran and Gabra groups in Kenya were restricted to separate areas in Marsabit District. A second group of Sabbo and Goona Oromo, also made up of Booran and Gabra groups, was cut off from the first and was moved in 1932 by the British administration to an area farther west, along the Waso Nyiro River to what is now Isiolo District. They are known today as the Waso Booran, after the name of the river along which they still live. In Ethiopia, both the Booran and Gabra groups of the Sabbo and Goona Oromo are collectively known as Booran. Today they inhabit the Sidamo Province of southern Ethiopia in the Boorana and Arero districts. Before 1910, however, when their territorial boundaries were restricted by the Abyssinian administration, they lived on both sides of the Gannale River and occupied parts of Jubaland in the vicinity of the Kawa and Gannale rivers in present-day

The land where the Booran live is hot and dry.

Somalia. Until very recently Oromo were known by the derogatory name of "Galla." They rejected this name in the 1960s, officially reclaiming the name Oromo.

The people known as the Booran today live on both sides of the Kenya-Ethiopia border and occupy a discontinuous territory stretching from the Gannale River in Ethiopia to the Waso Nyiro River in Kenya. Although the exact figures of Booran inhabiting this area is not known, it is thought they number about 1,000,000.▲

# chapter

# 2

# LAND AND LIVELIHOOD

**THE BOORAN SEE THEIR LAND AS DIVIDED INTO**
two parts, a highland region called Dirre and
Liban, and a lowland region called Golbo. Dirre
and Liban are situated in present-day Ethiopia.
For the Booran, they are the traditional centers
of culture and learning, and their most important ritual sites. The Golbo region corresponds
to the low-lying lands south of the Kenya-
Ethiopia border. The two regions are physically
separated by the Megaddo Escarpment, which
the Booran call Gorro.

The Booran distinguish three principal
landforms: *badda* or mountain and hills, *malbe*
or flats containing *goda* or depressions, and *booqe*
or salt lakes and pans.

The Booran believe that in this land the
creator Waaqa has provided them with plenty of
natural resources with which to make a living.

On this land, they say, can be found three categories of things: water and vegetation; domestic animals that depend on this water and vegetation; and human beings and other carnivorous animals who depend on the water, vegetation, and domestic animals.

The land inhabited by Booran is dry and hot. Water is essential not only for human life, but also for providing the grasses that keep their livestock from starvation. They distinguish three types of water: surface water that collects on the ground from rainfall (*lola*), man-made or natural dams (*harro*), and deep and shallow wells (*ella*). These wells are concentrated in over 35 different locations in Booranland. The most famous are known as the Tulla Saglaan, or the nine well complexes. Situated in Dirre, these wells are said to be ancient. The Booran consider themselves the present custodians of these wells, which were founded by their ancestors. The wells are an amazing technological achievement. They are the center of the Booran pastoral system.

Each well is surrounded by a grazing area. Within each grazing area are a number of *olla* or encampments. The typical *olla* consists of 15 to 30 households (*warra*), each with a male head or "father of the family" (*abba warraa*). Most wells, which are 65 to 98 feet deep, require between 10 and 60 people to operate them. The entire

Water, an essential part of life, can be difficult to come by in Booranland. Deep and shallow wells are scattered throughout the land. Many of the deep wells take several people to work. Cooperation between villages is necessary not only to get the water, but in governing water use.

*olla* must cooperate with neighbors in the watering of the herds and observe the correct rules governing the use of well water. Grazing, watering, and other activities are also coordinated with several members of society. The heads of the units are the main decision-makers. *Olla* in the same vicinity cluster together to form districts (*reera*), which in turn link to form neighborhoods (*arda*). Groups of *arda* together form a grazing range (*deeda*).

The supply of dry-season well water in Booranland allows the people to have a more settled existence and to cultivate some crops. Maize, sorghum, millet, or beans are grown in small plots in the encampments to supplement the diet of milk and meat. Crop and livestock production complement each other. Compared to the lowland Gabra camel-herders, who are constantly on the move in search of pasture for their camels and small stock, the Booran cattle-herders do not have to move very far from the main settlement.

Like the Gabra, however, the Booran also split the cattle and small stock herd into two groups: The main (*warra*, literally "home") herd is made up of milk-bearing animals that are kept close to the main settlement to provide nourishment for the family. The rest of the herd is kept in satellite camps (*fora*) farther afield. The herd is split this way to avoid draining the water sup-

*A young Booran girl begins weaving a basket for holding and carrying water.*

ply and grazing places close to the settlement. The Booran have earned a reputation for their skill as pastoralists and for their able management of the natural resources of their land. They have taken measures to safeguard and preserve

Booran woman laying the foundation to build a house.

the collective resources. Once every eight years an "assembly of the multitudes" (*gumii*) is held at the well-site of Ell Dallo to discuss issues relating to the fine balance that must be maintained among people, livestock, pasture, and water in the arid and semiarid region in which they live.

The Booran have a profound knowledge of their vegetation, recognizing about 400 species of plants. They classify these plants into two main categories: trees and shrubs (*muka*), and grasses (*buyyo*). Over 200 species of plants are gathered for a great variety of uses: as fuel, as building material, for making items such as stools, herding sticks, and ritual objects; for the preparation of medicine; for food, in the form of berries, edible roots, and chewing gum; as incense for the fumigation of milk containers and as perfume for women; as dyes for skins and containers. Plants are important in ceremonies. The fig tree in the highlands and the *Acacia tortilis* tree in the lowlands figure prominently in the myths and rites of all Booran. The Booran in the Dirre region use thirty varieties of grass and herbs as food for their cattle.

The breed of cattle kept by the Booran is known as the East African zebu. This short-horn, humped species is highly resistant, able to withstand some of the many droughts and epidemics that have plagued this region throughout history. Like many other African pastoralists, however, the Booran have been greatly affected by the natural and man-made disasters that have devastated their herds over the last 100 years. A terrible rinderpest epidemic virtually destroyed their herds and those of many other pastoral populations in East and Northeast Africa in the 1890s. The epidemic was introduced into the country through the importation of infected stock from India to feed British troops. In one of the worst droughts of this century, in 1984–85, Booran in Ethiopia lost more than 40 percent of their breeding stock. Kenyan Booran lost almost 90 percent of their herds in some places in the 1992 drought. As a result of these losses many herders have become completely impoverished; of those, many have taken up cultivation

Many Booran were forced to leave their homeland in search of a means of survival after losing their cattle.

around the towns of Marsabit, Isiolo, and Sololo. Others migrate to the large towns, where they live in the urban slums.

### ▼ HELPING ONE ANOTHER ▼

In the past, the Booran were able to rebuild their lost herds and begin life again through an elaborate system of social welfare that employed both internal and external assistance networks. Because of the repeated losses they have suffered, however, these coping mechanisms can no longer function. Within the society, various types of social assistance were available to help individual owners recover from circumstances

31

such as raids, disease, or drought. Redistribution
of stock wealth from the rich to the poor also
took place through client relationships. One
such method was known as *dabarre*, meaning
"passing," a form of pastoral banking system
whereby the poorer herders cared for the surplus
animals of the rich in exchange for the milk
provided by the female stock. They were also
allowed to keep male calves of the female for
themselves, but the female calves belonged to
the owner or lender of the animal. Links were
also forged between the Booran pastoralists, the
Oromo Waata hunter-gatherer communities, and
neighboring agricultural communities such as
the Konso people of southern Ethiopia. Through
these alliances, the specialized food production
systems of each group could be tapped in times
of crisis to cover shortages.

   In times of plenty, these relationships served
as a means of trade and exchange of products as
well as of services. During the rinderpest epidemic, for instance, many Booran were able to
survive starvation only by eating the wild game
and plant foods given to them by the Waata
hunter-gatherers. These Waata Oromo occupy a
position apart in the society due to their occupa-
tion of hunting, tanning, and curing, as well as
metalworking and potting. With the agricultural
Konso, the Booran barter livestock produce such
as milk, meat, butter, and hides in exchange for

grain foods. The Konso have helped the Booran survive periodic droughts and food shortages.

Besides cattle and small stock such as sheep and goats, Booran also keep horses, mules, and donkeys as riding animals and beasts of burden. In the past, the Oromo were excellent horsemen, and all the wars they fought in the defense of their territory were carried out on horseback. To break their cavalry power and disarm them, British and Abyssinian colonial administrators confiscated the majority of their horses and mules.

The Booran are not only pastoralists. They also have a long history of farming. According to their own accounts, agriculture was introduced into their society over a thousand years ago.

### ▼ COMMUNITY LIFE ▼

In the Booran lifestyle, cooperation is essential. Whether living in cattle camps or in towns, the Booran nurture a strong sense of community. They assist and confer with each other on a daily basis, believing that if one community member is in trouble, it affects everybody. They also seek blessings from the elders daily.

This sense of unity is expressed in Booran rituals. Certain substances, such as milk, butter, tobacco, and coffee play a symbolic role in binding the community together.

Coffee (*buna*) is one of the indigenous crops of the Booran region. A number of myths surround its origins. According to one of these myths, the plant sprouted from the tears Waaqa shed at the death of man. It is therefore a symbol of man's resurrection and of everlasting life.

In all Booran rituals, a ceremony called *buna qalla* is performed. *Qalla* literally means "slaughtered." The name *buna qalla* describes the preparation of the coffee. The berries are first bitten open with the teeth and then roasted in hot butter mixed with herbs and spices. When the butter penetrates the pierced pod, it bursts open. For the Booran, this image is connected with the fertility of the earth and of women. As seeds burst open and flower in the soil, so women conceive and the womb bursts open to bring forth the new child.

The hot coffee and butter mixture is communally shared, and the beans are chewed by all the participants. Prayers are also said for peace, for an abundant harvest, and for the multiplication of stock and people.

### ▼ MARRIAGE ▼

Coffee and butter are also central to the Booran marriage ceremony. The greatest blessing for a Booran married couple is to have many healthy children. Therefore it is essential to con-

centrate on fertility from the first moment of the ritual.

This is seen in the ceremony of the piercing of the coffee berries. On this occasion, the groom sits on a stool outside the nuptial hut. The bride hands him a basket containing nine coffee berries and a spear anointed with butter. The groom pierces each of the berries with the spear.

After this, a ceremony known as *rakko* is performed. The bride-to-be enters the house, and the groom sacrifices a sheep with the spear at the threshold of the hut. The blood of the sheep is rubbed on the navel of the young bride, and prayers are said for her fertility. *Buna qalla* is then prepared by the groom's mother as she says the following prayer:

> O my coffee, give my son's wife plenty of
>     offspring;
> May she bear children;
> Give her long life;
> Give her good health;
> Give her lasting peace;
> O Waaqa, may she understand and enjoy my
>     words;
> May she understand and enjoy my son's
>     words;
> Give them children together.

The birth of the first son (the birth of a daughter is considered less significant) is a moment of great jubilation and celebration for the whole family, and the joy of the event is shared by the entire community. The more children a woman bears, the greater her status in society.

## ▼ MANHOOD ▼

For the Booran, killing and bearing are symbolically linked. They are considered complementary actions in the attainment of manhood and womanhood. Just as the woman symbolically dies in the act of giving birth and lives again through the child she has borne, so to be worthy of fathering a child, a man, too, must die a symbolic death and emerge reborn a hero.

In traditional Booran society, before the practice was banned by the government, this was done through the hunt.

Before he could marry, a man was expected to go into the wilderness and kill a big-game animal such as a buffalo, lion, rhino, elephant, or giraffe. On returning with his trophy, the man was celebrated for his prowess and skill as a hunter. His head was anointed with butter, and all the women present adorned him with their beaded necklaces. He was then eligible to wear special metal ornaments around his neck and arms, and an ostrich feather in his hair-band. At the ceremony, accompanied by his age-mates, he

A Booran woman who has many children is considered blessed.

strutted through the village and sang boastful songs recounting his exploits. Special tribute was paid to his mother on this occasion, in praise and thanks for the life she had given him.▲

# chapter

# 3

# HISTORY

THE BOORAN, LIKE ALL OTHER OROMO, USE the word *argaa-d'ageettii* to designate "history." *Argaa* means "that which is seen," and *d'ageettii* signifies those events that have been witnessed in the present and the events recorded in the oral traditions and handed down by word of mouth from the past. Oral historians and guardians of the oral traditions are known as *warra argaa d'ageettii*.

The Oromo believe that everything in the universe has a history, a point of origin in time and space, and that everything unfolds through this spectrum of time according to its own peculiar nature. The Oromo believe that history is a series of cyclical events, which are made up of different units of time. These build to make bigger and bigger cycles that form a spiral. The smallest unit of time is the cycle of one day

## WHY WAAQA WITHDREW FROM THE EARTH

Long ago, Waaqa was lying very close to the earth and people could ask him whatever they needed, and there was always plenty of rain.

Once upon a time, Waaqa sent for all the animals and said to them: "You can speak freely to me and even complain about those things which cause you to suffer." So the animals assembled before Waaqa.

The first animal summoned by Waaqa to speak was the donkey. The donkey stepped forward and said: "O Waaqa, you asked me to speak, but I have only to thank you. I have no cause for complaint."

Then came the horse. The horse, too, behaved very respectfully toward Waaqa. "I have only thanks to offer you," he said. "Thanks for the grass you give me to eat, for the water you give me to drink, and for your sun that warms me."

And all the other animals spoke in this way.

Finally, it was the mule's turn. The mule complained. She said, "O Waaqa, you ordered me to speak up. All right, I do have a cause for complaint. You are lying with your belly too close to the earth. It is raining far too much." And while speaking in this vein, she grew more and more angry, until she kicked Waaqa in the belly.

At that, Waaqa withdrew upward from the earth. He withdrew from all of us, but he abandoned the mule in a special way: from that day onward, the mule was unable to bear young.

marked by the rising and setting of the sun; days add up to form one lunar month, marked by the rising and setting of the moon; months add up to form a year, marked by the cycle of the four seasons through the solar year; eight years form a cycle based on the time that power is held successively by the five groups in society during one generation of 40 years. When these 40-generation power-cycles return nine times, one era of time elapses. This revolution of the 360-year cycle of time is known as a *jaatama*, or an era.

The term *jaatama* is derived from the Oromo word for the number 60. At the completion of every *jaatama*, therefore, a new beginning has to be marked in the cycle of time. This new beginning is thought to be a time of great crisis. Society can no longer continue to operate according to the same rules and to function in the same way. The entire social, political, and economic order of life has to be radically changed and undergo a major transformation. This notion of crisis is termed *sagli* in Oromo. *Sagli* is the word for the number nine and can be seen as representing the beginning point of a new cycle. Crises occur at every critical turning point in time, but with differing degrees of intensity. Thus when one *jaatama* is itself repeated nine times, the Oromo believe there occurs a major catastrophe, not only within their society but on a world scale.

Expert time-reckoners are assigned to com-

Some Booran have managed to retain a traditional lifestyle.

pute the different cycles. The work of the historian, on the other hand, is to keep a record of the events that take place within each of the cycles and to be able to interpret them in the light of past cycles. These events are not seen as isolated incidents, but as repetitions of events that have already occurred. These levels of events are interconnected, forming a spiraling system.

According to an elder, the present crisis of the Oromo, which began 100 years ago during the colonial period, is a time of transformation marking the return to an ancient cycle of time in the history of the Oromo people, relinking them to their origins. This ancient period of crisis is known as the Sagli of Horo, named after the first ancestor of the Oromo nation.▲

42

# chapter

# 4

# SOCIAL ORGANIZATION

**BEFORE THE BRITISH COLONIZED EASTERN**
Africa in the early 1800s, the traditional Oromo
system of government was founded on two separate but interlinked institutions, known as the
*Gada* and the *Qaalluu*. The *Gada* represented
political power, while the *Qaalluu* stood for religious authority.

In the past, each of the five territorial divisions of the Oromo elected its own regional
*Gada* political assembly for a period of eight
years. Before they could assume power, however,
the *Gada* leaders from all the regions had to
make a pilgrimage to the ritual center of the
*Abba Mudaa*. The *Abba Mudaa*, literally meaning "Father of Anointment," was placed at the
center of the five regions to mediate and admin-
ister the judicial, political, and spiritual order of
the Oromo nation. During the colonial period,

the regional *Gada* were systematically stripped of
their power and rendered obsolete. In the remote
regions of southern Ethiopia and northern Kenya,
among the Sabbo and Goona Booran and Gabra,
however, the *Gada* and *Qaalluu* have survived
fairly intact. Although in the modern states of
Ethiopia and Kenya today they no longer have a
political function, the rituals associated with
them continue to be performed and kept alive.
Every eight years, Booran in southern Ethiopia
and northern Kenya still elect *Gada* assemblies
and make a pilgrimage to receive blessings from
the Sabbo *Qaalluu*. The last such celebrations
were held in 1987.

The origins of the *Gada* and *Qaalluu* institutions are too far in the past to be known, but
different versions of them were widely practiced
by many other peoples in the Horn of Africa.
Although the *Gada* was a means for regulating
power, it was more than a political system. The
institution is derived from the underlying prin-
ciple of time, by which the entire society was
organized. This concept, at the heart of all
Oromo thought and culture, is called *ayyaana*.
*Ayyaana* is an extremely difficult concept to
define, but it can be described as a classification
device. According to *ayyaana*, everything in the
Oromo cultural universe was structured in space
and time. It was on the basis of this concept that
the whole *Gada* system operated. *Gada* encom-

The oldest girl usually helps out by taking care of the younger children in the family.

passed the whole society, structuring the lives of all the members of the community as they passed through the different stages of the life-cycle from birth to death.

As a system of power, *Gada* was also highly reputed for its egalitarian and democratic nature. As we have seen, the division of the society into elder and younger brothers marks social, economic, political, and ritual differences that are inherently unjust to the younger, less privileged men. To counteract these inequalities, the ancient *Gada* system created an ingenious means of regulating power so that it was more equal. One way in which this system operated was through the *Qaalluu* institution.

The *Qaalluu* are shaman priests mythologically connected to the High *Qaalluu* or *Abba Mudaa*. This first *Qaalluu* is said to have descended from heaven in a cloud of mist and to have been "found" by a Waata Oromo hunter-gatherer. In many versions of the myth recounting his descent among men, he is described as wearing a black and white spotted turban on his head, an iron horn-shaped ornament on his forehead, and iron bracelets on his upper arm. He carried a rhino whip, a wooden staff, and a metal drum. He also had a container filled with spitting cobras. A black and white spotted cow was found with him. The Booran offered the *Qaalluu* milk to drink and a young woman to be his bride. In this way the mysterious and holy

personage came to be adopted and to live among the Oromo. He is seen as a universal figure and son of all men (*Ilm Namaa*).

It is the descendant of this first *Qaalluu* to whom pilgrimage was made in the past for blessing by the elected leaders of all the five political assemblies of the *Gada*. In each of these regional assemblies there were also minor or lesser *Qaalluu* representing the spiritual authority of the *Abba Mudaa*. This was known as the *Qaalluu* institution.

There were five *Qaalluu* institutions in each of the Oromo groups. Unlike in the *Gada*, where the political leader was elected for a period of eight years, the position of *Qaalluu* passed from father to son. In the *Gada*, the political officers were drawn from the ranks of the elder sons, while the *Qaalluu* were the youngest sons of the second or younger wife of the *Qaalluu*. The *Gada* represented the temporal authority of the Booran, while the *Qaalluu* represented the spiritual authority of the Gabaro. The roles of the elder and younger sons were ritually reversed because all the political power of the elder group was granted to them with the permission of the younger, spiritual group. In Oromo, *Gada* is associated with male values and attributes: strength, virility, prowess in war, and strong leadership. The *Qaalluu* on the other hand stands for feminine values: peace, plenty, and fertility. The *Qaalluu* did not engage in combat.

## OROMO PROVERBS

Gurraaf garaan walii nyaapha.
The ear and the stomach are enemies.
(A stomach will growl when it's hungry, no matter what you're
   trying to listen to.)

Cubbuun infurfursit duraan, inquallifitti boodan.
Sin makes one fat, and then makes one thin.
(Evil behavior may bring advantages right away, but you'll pay in
   the end.)

Manni abbaan hin oolchin hattuu oolcha.
The house owner didn't take care of his house, so the thief "took
   care" of it.
(Protect your possessions if you want to keep them.)

Harren gowwaan waraabessa gaggeessitti.
The foolish donkey walks the hyena home.
(A fool gets hurt by helping his enemy.)

Kan akka bulti hin beekne, akka jechaa hin walaaltu.
She who doesn't know how to live sure knows how to talk about
   living!
(Know-it-alls really know the least of all.)

Biyya goophoon baayyatett, isa ol jedhee deemutu fokkisa.
In a land with lots of hunchbacks, a straight-backed person
   looks ugly.
(Opinions differ depending on the surroundings.)

Quufaan, Waaqqatti darbata.
A satisfied man throws things at God.
(It's easy to be arrogant when you have everything you want.)

Kan jige hindeebihu, han duhe hinkahu.
That which fell over will not return, and he who dies will not live
   again.
(What's done is done.)

This role reversal was part of the system of balance that operated at all levels of the power structure. All of Booran society was based on this dichotomy between the firstborn and the younger sons. Both institutions therefore complemented one another, just as husband and wife complement one another in a Booran family. It ensured that power was equally distributed.

Power was also distributed through alternation. All of Oromo society was divided into halves called *moieties*. These halves represented the right- and left-hand sides of the social body. The right-hand half was considered the senior *moiety*, or Booran, and the left was the junior, or Barrentu. The right hand was the male element, and the left was thought to be female. In order to balance power between the two halves of the nation, power shifted from one to the other.

Succession was also used to distribute power among all the members of society. This was done through the *luba* system. All the males born into one generation (within the same 40-year period) belonged to the same generation group. This group was divided into five sets, called *luba*, which performed all the ceremonies marking the different stages of the life cycle. Power passed from one *luba* to another, each assuming power for a period of eight years, then handing over power to the following *luba*.

Children learn their roles in society by doing tasks from a young age.

Among the Sabbo and Goona, there are five *Qaalluu* clans, four belonging to the Sabbo and one to the Goona (junior) *moiety*. These *Qaalluu* clans oversee the council of electors who are responsible for blessing and installing the new *Abba Gadaa* into office. They do not participate in the election process and are therefore neutral figures, representing divine authority. Booran continue to rotate power between the different *luba* and to perform all the rites and rituals associated with the different stages in the life cycle. There are ten such stages, through which men pass every eight years. The periods pass from grades of boyhood, to junior warriorhood; then the men become political leaders and finally retire and dedicate themselves to spiritual matters.▲

# chapter

# 5

# RELIGION AND WORLDVIEW

**BOORAN BELIEVE IN ONE CREATOR OF THE** world, whom they call Waaqa Tokkicha, "the one god." This creator is also frequently referred to as Waaqa *guraacha*, "black god." The adjective *gurraacha* stands for the idea of absolute origin, the ultimate source of all things. The word carries in it the sense of mystery, that which is still in the shadow, or is not yet revealed.

Writers on the Oromo have often portrayed Waaqa as a Sky God. Although the Oromo look upward when referring to their creator, they do not confuse him with the sky. The Oromo believe that there are seven skies above and below the earth. It is generally believed that Waaqa is found beyond these seven skies.

The traditional Oromo believed that it was Waaqa who created heaven and earth and all that is found in them. In the Oromo view of their creator, Waaqa is at the same time one and many. These multiple aspects of the supreme deity are designated by the word *ayyaana*.

Although primarily a device for computing time, *ayyaana* is also a rudimentary form of science and a classification tool. It provides a mental framework according to which all social, cultural, and natural phenomena are codified and classified. It is the model according to which the forces of chaos, order, and change are explained and understood.

*Ayyaana* is also believed to mold the destiny of all things. This destiny is believed to live in the soul at birth. It is guided by the actual moment at which all things come into the world, as well as the relationship of this soul to all other souls that share this time of birth. In this regard, an animal, a plant, and a person that come into existence at the same time have something profoundly in common and their fates are believed to be intertwined.

In the Oromo scheme, destiny is a spiral, like the events of history. One's personal destiny cannot be separated from that of the period of time into which one is born. Destiny thus functions at many different levels. Fate is lived out on the personal as well as the collective level. The cycle of an individual life is embedded in the cycles of the universe; it is inscribed into the cycle of human, natural, and cosmic history,

According to Oromo philosophy, a person cannot separate his destiny from the period in which he is born.

into the fate of the family, the country, and the world it is born into. All these concentric circles that make up the movement of time are individually and collectively known as *ayyaana*.

*Ayyaana* is essentially a religious idea that tries to explain the origin of the universe, the nature of the laws that govern it, the relationship between the creator and the created, and the fundamental problem of the one and the many. In the Oromo religion everything flows out of Waaqa, in the form of rays of energy. Through this radiance everything comes into being. As the One dissolves, the light is diffused into multiple directions. The entire world thus becomes a reflection of this unity, acquiring its own indi-

53

vidual soul or essence while remaining part of the greater soul. These pathways of creation are also known as *ayyaana. Ayyaana* is the spiritual origin of the universe and stands for the principles of unity and diversity underlying all creation.

The Oromo believe that there was a time when Waaqa drew away from man, corresponding to the origins of sin, which causes catastrophes such as drought, disease, and war. For the world to prosper and flourish in spite of these calamities, the Oromo believe that distance and respect must be kept between all things. The idea of distance and respect is connected to a concept called *saffu. Saffu,* or "the sense of harmony," directs one on the right path. It shows the way in which life can be best lived, and gives a sense of order. It is an ideal toward which the Oromo always strive.

## ▼ PEACE IN THE WORLD ▼

There cannot be order in the world without peace. Maintaining peace is a pervasive aspect in the lives of all Oromo. This is known as the Peace of the Booran (*Nagaya Booraana*). The Booran work toward peace constantly. The elders are in charge of keeping it, and every member of the community seeks it with prayers and blessings. The Booran believe that if peace is destroyed, so is the order of the universe.

Prayers are said for peace at every undertaking made by the Booran. Their daily greetings and activities revolve around the idea of peace and prayers. They are said when the cattle set out from their kraals in the morning and when they return in the evenings. The Oromo believe that no one should go to bed "with anger in his belly." Earthly peace is ultimately represented in the *Qaalluu,* who acts as the mediator between humankind and Waaqa.

Booran usually worship in high places, on mountains and hilltops, or under sacred trees. They perform sacrifices of sheep, goats, and cattle. Ritual substances such as myrrh and roasted coffee beans also figure in all their religious celebrations. When making a sacrifice they face east, in the direction of the rising sun.

The Booran believe that when they die, they rejoin all their dead forefathers and foremothers in a place called *Iddo-Dhugga,* the "place of truth," where grass is always green, where cattle are fat and healthy, and where milk flows.▲

# CONCLUSION

**TODAY, NOT ALL BOORAN LIVE IN GRASS HUTS** in cattle camps. Over the past 100 years, their ancient way of life has undergone profound change. While their fathers still eke out a living with herds diminished by drought, disease, and war or are reduced to working for low wages as guards and sentries in the homes of the wealthy in large towns, a few privileged young men and women have been able to get an education. Some have even been able to go to college, and a few find employment in the government and other offices or engage in business.

But because of their isolation from mainstream development, the large majority of the Booran still live according to their traditions. Although many have converted to Christianity and Islam, they still practice their traditional religion and perform sacrifices for peace, plenty, and rain at different times of the year. However, they say that Waaqa cannot hear their prayers because they no longer pray with one voice. They feel that this lack of unity explains their present predicament.

Although they know that the real seats of power in modern times are the national governments of Ethiopia and Kenya, the Booran continue to celebrate the *Gada* rituals. From their

56

Today the Booran face the challenge of combining traditional culture with modern culture. Some have met this challenge by moving to larger cities, such as Addis Ababa, Ethiopia.

elders, the Booran derive the strength to face troubled times and find comfort and hope for the future in their wise counsel. In fact, so important is the influence of the *Gada* leaders among all the Oromo people today, that a retired Booran *Abba Gadaa* was assassinated by opponents of the Oromo in 1994 for his outspoken criticism of the new regime that was instituted in Ethiopia in 1992.

For the past 30 years, the Oromo of Ethiopia have been fighting a guerrilla war for the liberation and self-determination of their people. During this time, thousands of Oromo have been tortured, imprisoned, and executed. This persecution has forced many other thousands into exile all over the world. Yet their sense of identity remains strong, and most Oromo yearn to return to their homeland.

According to the Booran elders, the present times represent a state of disorder and confusion, not only for the Oromo people, but for the world as a whole. As the millennium draws to a close, they believe that a major crisis is at hand. Like other native peoples, they predict that the present world order is coming to a painful and dramatic end. According to this prophecy, only the righteous will be saved from the cataclysm. But those who survive and emerge from the crisis will live in a better, more just and humane world. ▲

# Glossary

**Abba Mudaa** "Father of anointment," the central *Qaalluu* or spiritual leader, who acts as an arbiter among the five political districts of Oromoland.

**argaa-d'ageettii** Oromo oral "history."

**ayyaana** The Oromo concept of time and cycles, governing their entire worldview.

**Barrentu** Eastern Oromo groups.

**Booran** Among Oromo peoples, the firstborn son of a family and the senior, elite section of society. Western Oromo groups.

**Booran guutuu** "Pure" Booran, or those eldest sons qualified to wear signs of their elite status.

**Cushitic, Eastern** The language family to which the Oromo dialects belong.

**dabarre** "Passing," a way to redistribute wealth. Poor people care for the cattle of rich people, and may keep some of the young.

**Gabaro (Gabra)** All Oromo sons who are not firstborn. Also refers to a particular section of the Oromo created during colonial times.

**Gada** The traditional Oromo political assembly, made up of elected officials.

**Horo** The first ancestor, or founder, of the Oromo nation.

*jaatama* A 360-year cycle or era.

*luba* Age set; there are five *luba* in each 40-year generation of men, and power is passed from one *luba* to the next.

**Nagaya Booraana** Peace of the Booran. A state of order and harmony in the universe for which the Booran constantly strive in their daily lives.

**Oromo** The ancient name of the people whom British colonial governments pejoratively termed "Galla," and who were artificially divided into separate groups.

**Qaalluu** The institution of Oromo religious leaders.

*sagli* A time of crisis, when a cycle in history concludes and begins again.

**Tulla Saglaan** The nine well complexes that form the center of Oromo pastoral society and symbolize the power of the ruling group.

**Waaqa** The Oromo creator or god.

# For Further Reading

Alberro, M. "The Booran cattle and their tribal owners." *World Animal Review*, Jan.-Mar. 57, pp. 30–57, 1986.

Bahrey. "History of the Galla," in D.Levine, ed. *History of the Galla (Oromo) of Ethiopia.* Oakland: Sun Publishing, 1993.

Bartels, L. *Oromo Religion: Myths and Rites of the Western Oromo of Ethiopia.* Berlin: Dietrich Reimer, 1983.

Baxter, P.T.W., and Almagor, U., eds. *Age, Generation, and Time. Some Features of East African Age Organizations.* London: C Hurst, 1978.

Cotter, George. *Proverbs and Sayings of the Oromo People of Ethiopia and Kenya, with English Translations.* Queenston, Ontario: Edwin Mellen, 1992.

Dahl, G., and Megerssa, G. "The Sources of life: Booran concepts of wells and water," in G. Palsson, ed. *From Water to World-Making.* Uppsala: Scandinavian Institute of African Studies, 1990.

Kassam, A. and Megerssa, G. "Iron and beads: Male and female symbols of creation," in I. Hodder, ed. *The Meaning of Things: Material Culture and Symbolic Expression*. London: Allen and Unwin, 1989.

Legesse, A. Gada: *Three Approaches to the Study of African Society*. New York: Free Press, 1973.

# Index

ABOUT THE AUTHOR

Dr. Gemetchu Megerssa was born in Ethiopia and belongs to the Macha Oromo group of Western Ethiopia. He has spent a lifetime learning the oral traditions, culture, and history of the Oromo people, both from family members and through his own studies among the Booran Oromo. Dr. Megerssa received his doctorate in Anthropology based on a thesis about the Oromo.

Dr. Megerssa is currently continuing the study of his own people.

PHOTO CREDITS

p. 57 © AP/Wide World; all other photos © CFM, Nairobi

EDITORIAL CONSULTANT

Aneesa Kassam, Ph.D.

DESIGN

Kim Sonsky